BMW

THE BOOK OF THE CAR

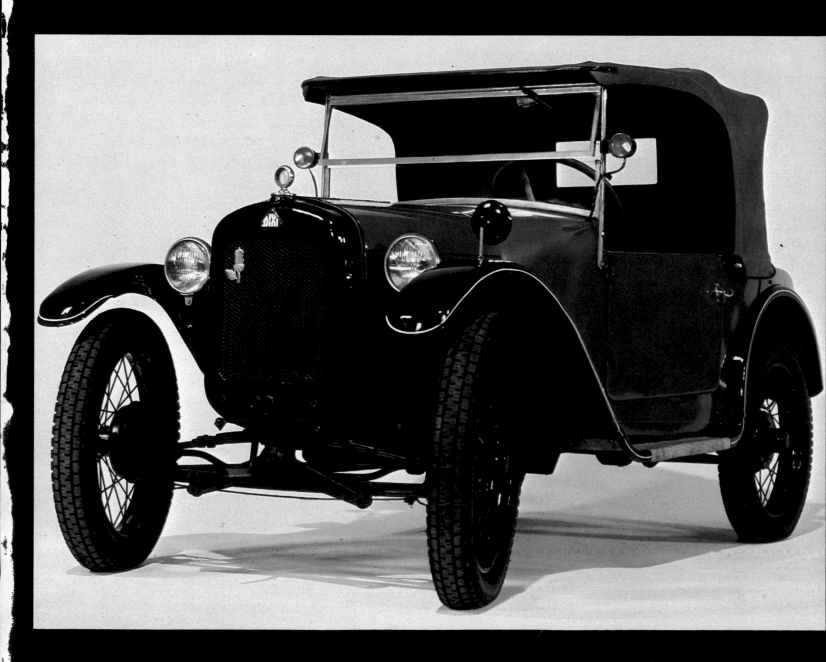

BMW

THE BOOK OF THE CAR

DON SLATER

GALLERY BOOKS

Published by Gallery Books
A division of W.H. Smith Publishers Inc.,
112, Madison Avenue,
New York, New York 10016.

Printed in Spain by Graficromo s.a.

Produced by Winchmore Publishing Services Limited
40 Triton Square
London NW1

Edited by Catherine Bradley
Designed by Roy Williams
Typeset by SX Composing, Rayleigh, Essex

ISBN 0-8317-0900-6

CONTENTS

Today, BMW cars project a strong image: they are an integrated range of high performance, well-engineered, quality cars. BMW cars are small and on the sporty side, but immensely practical and solid. They are a status symbol – and as immediately recognizable as a status symbol must be – but with a cool and understated manner. They carry price tags which mark them as luxury cars but neither wastefully extravagant nor frivolous. The buyer, or admirer from a distance, knows that behind these cars stands a huge reputation for engine design and racing success.

Yet this image is only 20 years old. For BMW, alone among today's automotive giants, came into its own after the postwar boom was already advanced. Before the company's final escape from the jaws of bankruptcy in 1959, BMW's image consisted only of its reputation for engineering and racing and its production of several classic cars. But its classics (the 328 and the 507, for example) always had small and financially insignificant production runs. BMW's standard models, which only sold well in the late 1930s, were generally huge, over-powered, and over-priced. The company was largely sustained by the production of other goods – notably motorcycles and aircraft engines – and by its periodic success with cheap cars that were a million miles away from BMW's quality image (the Austin Seven and the Isetta). This was a company led by engineers in pursuit of design perfection rather than by people who could direct the development of a line of cars that would sell. Between its huge clunkers and its cheap mass vehicles, BMW suffered for over 60 years from a blind spot for the one product band which would finally give the company stability and dramatic success: a series of mid-range cars for the monied middle class who could both appreciate and afford what BMW was doing.

The story of BMW, then, is a story of failures as much as of ultimate success, of false starts and missed opportunities, of beautiful machines and great white elephants. But above all it is the story of the central drama of 20th-century industry: the struggle to bring technology and marketing into dialogue, to harness the enormous expertise in modern engineering to a sense of what consumers want, to make good machines which sell.

CHAPTER 1

THE FACTORY AT EISENACH

The history of BMW cars up to the Second World War is essentially the story of a factory at Eisenach (now East Germany). Although this plant changed hands several times before its products actually bore the name of Bayerische Motoren Werke, it was here that the reputation of BMW cars was forged. The Eisenach factory produced motor cars from 1896 through its takeover by BMW in 1928 to the beginning of the Second World War. After the war, when BMW had to rebuild itself from the very little that was left, Eisenach was nationalized by East Germany and the story moves on to Munich.

The Eisenach factory came into being as part of a major economic feat: the rapid and explosive industrialization of Germany in the last decades of the 19th century. Its founder, Heinrich Ehrhardt, was symbolic of the period. Born in 1840 to a peasant family in Thuringia, Ehrhardt developed a flair for invention which he directed into engineering for heavy industrial products in leading economic sectors: railroads, containers, metal work, and pumps. He worked with and established several firms all over Germany before returning to his native Thuringia in 1896, where he decided to set himself up in the latest growth sector of the economy, vehicle production, then being revolutionized by the internal combustion engine and the development of the horseless carriage. On 22 December 1896 Ehrhardt officially registered the Fahrzeugfabrik Eisenach (Eisenach Vehicle Factory), with himself as major stockholder.

Two features of the company were indicative of the still-unformed and unspecialized nature of the industry at that time. First, the factory was more in the nature of a large workshop so that, although it employed over 600 people by the end of its first year, it still bore little resemblance to the highly mechanized and streamlined production process associated with the automotive industry. Secondly, it was not a

Left: In 1898 Eisenach obtained a license to produce a motorcar design owned by the Société Decauville. The company successfully continued to produce Decauville voiturettes like this one until 1903.

Right: An early Wartburg (1899), with unsprung rear axle and tiller steering.

car factory but a vehicles factory, simultaneously producing gun carriages, military vehicles, bicycles, electrical vehicles, and cars with gasoline engines. The range of vehicles produced for individual consumers alone during the first years shows that 'automobiles' did not yet refer to a specific idea of a vehicle differentiated from the others. For example, for its first eight years the firm did not decide finally between electricity and gasoline as fuel, electricity being considered more suitable for taxis. Furthermore, the break with the notion of the horseless carriage had decidedly not yet been made: the Wartburg Electric, made from 1899 to 1902, looked ready to be hitched up to a team of horses. Eisenach's first motor car production range (first shown at Dusseldorf in 1898) was suitably varied: a three-wheel voiturette, an electric coach and a private car with a two-cylinder gasoline engine.

In fact, motorcars were a liability for Fahrzeugfabrik Eisenach during its first years, its main income being from munitions wagons and bicycles. Ehrhardt, however, was convinced of the future of automobile production and decided to cut through the trial-and-error path being pursued by his own design department by buying a design under license. In September 1898, therefore, Ehrhardt signed a contract with the Société Decauville, giving his firm the right to produce the 3.5-hp Decauville voiturette and to export it throughout Europe and North America.

The first of these cars was produced by Christmas and bore the brand name of Wartburg, named, like Ehrhardt's bicycles, after the castle overlooking Eisenach. The Wartburg looked very like a horsedrawn carriage, a two-seater with steering by tiller and back-mounted engine. However, it was a light car with a good two-cylinder, 3–4hp air-cooled engine which could get up to 31 mph (50 km/h). Its rear axle was unsprung, but it had an advanced front suspension system. Another

version was introduced soon after, this time with a water-cooled engine capable of putting out 5hp. The car attracted considerable attention throughout Germany. However, car sales were still not a good earner for the company and, as bicycle and military sales fell off, the firm approached crisis; by 1903 it was in the red. The Eisenach design team made many improvements on the Decauville design, and added to their sales program such ploys as a portable garage, included as an optional extra. In 1902, they introduced an 8.5-hp car which was more in the image of the automobile to come. They also devoted much energy to racing, which remained a major form of advertising throughout the history of BMW.

Ehrhardt continued to invest in the business until 1903, developing a car with a four-cylinder engine on a tubular frame, but in that year he pulled out of the firm to look after his other business interests (taking with him the Decauville license). Fahrzeugfabrik Eisenach remained, however, saddled with debts and bereft of its major automotive product, and came under the control of the engineer Willy Seck. Seck and his team took the best option open to them and devoted their energies to producing a single model, fully designed and produced in their factory.

The new car was called the Dixi, Latin for 'I have spoken,' and foreshadowed the advertiser's perennial claim to be offering 'the last word' in cars. The name and the car clearly reflected the firm's attitude toward the market: it was produced in small numbers and sold at a premium price derived from high engineering standards and the use of top-quality materials. First shown in 1904, the Dixi was introduced in three versions. First came the S6, with a two-cylinder, 8hp engine. The T7, the smallest Dixi car, was powered by a one-cylinder, 1200cc engine yielding 7–9hp and a maximum speed of 25 mph (40 km/h), which – along with its two-speed gearbox — was housed in the body of a two-seater spider. Pictures of its hard-top version show again the uncertainty of what was wanted in a car: though fully three-quarters open to the elements on both sides, the hard-top came with curtains and roll-shade for privacy or style. Eisenach produced 60 of these cars. The Ts came out with several different engine designs, but production numbers were very low indeed. Only the S12 and very similar S14 — also introduced in 1904 — sold over 100 cars: this had a four-cylinder, 3.5-liter engine and overhead camshaft, which put out 16hp. It had universal transmission and was built in many forms: saloon, coupé, convertible, landau and taxi. It also cost twice the price of a T7.

The Dixi gave the firm an excellent reputation for achieving good performance and reliability. However, Eisenach was not yet producing many cars. Presaging themes which were to dominate the firm throughout its career, its engineers were making technical advances with wonderful regularity but were inducing the company to produce a welter of different models, all highly-priced and with low production runs. This

was exacerbated in the early years (right through 1927) by the still craft-oriented nature of coach-building: a very large proportion of the cars were virtually individually-customized artefacts. This meant either contracting-out coachwork, or concentrating much skilled labor in the factory: either way it meant high costs and restriction of sales to an exclusive luxury market.

Thus it was not until after the 1907–08 recession that the firm actually picked itself up off the financial floor, aided by its first biggish seller, the Dixi R8 (650 produced), a small and light four-cylinder, 14hp car. Typically for Eisenach, the R8's sporting successes led to its commercial success, and its sports two-seater version was especially popular. Eisenach developed its small R series into several popular lines in the prewar period. As the world headed for war, Fahrzeugfabrik Eisenach went into the boom-time, producing many different models including another relative best-seller, the S16, a 32-hp model which rang up 710 cars from 1912 to 1925.

With its automobile production finally off the ground, the

Left: The Dixi T7 was the smallest Dixi produced by Eisenach. It was the beginning of the firm's reputation for sound and reliable design.

Above: Dixi made a wide variety of commercial and special purpose vehicles. This ambulance was a 14hp Dixi.

Below: The R8 was Dixi's first large selling car and was developed into a long line of cars.

Eisenach factory was brought to a standstill by the First World War. It was turned over to military production and virtually disappeared in the aftermath of the war, when it was dismantled by the Allied Control Commission. Production was not resumed until the end of 1919, with two prewar Dixi models. The first postwar model did not come out of the factory until 1921; the Dixi G1, a 6/18hp, four-cylinder which was very large and expensive. It was also produced in more powerful racing versions.

By May 1921 Fahrzeugfabrik Eisenach (generally known as the Dixi Werke) was plunging into the financial abyss of the German economic crisis and was probably only saved by a very unequal merger with the Gothaer Waggonfabrik. There was a considerable loss of independence involved, clearly shown in the company's new policy of producing a very small number of models in contrast with its previous profusion of

Right: The 3/15 Dixi reestablished Eisenach both as a car producer and as an international racer: Dixis racing on the Avus track in September 1928.

Below: Dixis participating in the June 1928 ADAC 3000-km Alpine Tour.

designs and modifications. It was not an effective policy; the firm continued to concentrate (like many other European manufacturers) on large and expensive cars, well-designed and good performers. However, they were priced for a market which did not actually exist — and least of all in Germany, suffering throughout the 1920s from depression, unemployment, inflation, and chronic instability among the only class that could potentially afford to buy Eisenach's Dixis. For example, Dixi's major car of the 1920s, the G2 6/24 (produced 1923 to 1928), incorporated important engineering advances and was impressive in competition, but sold very little. In 1926 Dixi introduced the hugely expensive six-cylinder P1/P2 into the already overcrowded luxury class and got nowhere. At the same time, they had designed a small car but did not manage to get it into production.

On the one hand, Dixi was caught in a general economic crisis: even its holding company, Gothaer, could offer little help when its own production was being drastically curtailed. On the other, Dixi was not alone among European automobile manufacturers, seemingly unable to grow up and out of the logic of early car production into the new world of Ford's assembly line, standard models, low prices and mass marketing. Germany was swamped with American imports and Dixi — again, not alone — took refuge in the sinking ship of luxury cars.

By 1927, the situation was again critical and decisive measures were needed. Jakob Schapiro, who had engineered the Gothaer takeover, stepped in again, putting the Eisenach factory together with another of his interests, the Cyklon plant in Mylau. Together they produced a Cyklon model as the Dixi 9/40hp. Though low-priced for its class, it was still a big six-cylinder model and in the event was a disaster.

Well on their way to bankruptcy, compounded by the threatened crumbling of Schapiro's entire automotive empire, Eisenach was urged to proceed as quickly as possible with the production of a small and cheap car which might rescue all their fortunes. In fact they could not move fast enough, and a rescue was attempted by the same method which had established the company's fortunes in the first place: licensed production of a proven foreign car. They chose a winner, the

The little 3/15 Dixi DA-1 was a dependable, versatile and affordable car for the German middle classes. It helped BMW to weather the economic depression and emerge in the early 1930s as a major motor manufacturer.

two-seater 'Baby' Austin Seven. A small car, with an output of 10.5hp, economical gasoline consumption and — most importantly — selling for little more than a high-priced motorcycle, it had already been enormously successful in Britain and its license was being vied for by several German manufacturers.

Schapiro won the license for Eisenach and the first model was off the assembly line in September 1927 as the Dixi 3/15 DA 1 ('DA' denoting 'German version'). It was an immediate and substantial top seller of continuous appeal which carried

the company right through to the mid-1930s. For Schapiro, however, the story did not have such a happy engine. Despite his success in Eisenach, Schapiro was still under constant financial pressure, with the rest of his holdings in a rocky state. He finally had to sell Dixi Werke in 1928, finding a willing purchaser in the noted motorcycle and aircraft engine manufacturer, the Bayerische Motoren Werke. All this turned out to be a prelude to his total withdrawal from the automobile business.

Thus it was that in 1928, the original Fahrzeugfabrik

Eisenach — finally on its way to financial health — changed its name to BMW. The white and blue BMW emblem — designed in 1919 as a stylized representation of an airplane propeller at full throttle — would appear on its motor cars from now on.

Above: The Dixi DA-1 was built in a number of body styles, but the one pictured above was in fact a custom-made body built by the coachmakers Büschel.

Right: Like much commercial design of the period, the famous BMW emblem drew on the best of contemporary art: a futurist version of a propeller in motion.

CHAPTER 2

THE RISE
OF BMW

While the Eisenach story symbolizes the risky and uncertain adventure of early automobile production, the history of BMW itself symbolizes another important strand of industrial development closely related to automotives: again, the company was established by a mixed bag of engineering adventurers and financial entrepreneurs chasing potentially huge profits in new growth sectors. However, this time the field was aviation engines, and the step to success was profit from war production.

The kernel of BMW was the Karl Rapp Motorenwerke Munchen GmbH, founded in 1913 by the engineer Karl Rapp and the financier Auspitzer. It started off as a very small workshop which was attempting to design an aircraft engine that could win competitions: this was considered the surest route to government and commercial contracts. It was completely unsuccessful in this endeavor until the war overtook it: precisely because of its lack of success, it had excess plant capacity available to undertake the war production which had to spring into existence immediately following July 1914. Contracts from Prussia and Austro-Hungary followed immediately. Technical problems with Rapp's engines in the form of bad vibration threatened the new contracts but, in the first flush of success, Rapp's business manager, Max Wiedmann, nonetheless undertook a massive expansion program. This included the setting-up of a Vienna office in collaboration with the financier Castiglioni.

Despite this expansion, business was not good, cash shortages were endemic and product complaints continued. Castiglioni, with his finger on Austrian aircraft engine contracts, was eager to step in and was firmly in control by 1916. He brought with him a contract for 200 Austro-Daimler engines, an engine being pushed by a young Austrian flight officer, Franz-Joseph Popp. Popp was not only an engineer but a very canny manager. He went to Munich to oversee production of his engine at the Rapp works and stayed on to pull the company into shape. Popp was to remain at BMW until the Second World War, overseeing its moves into motorcycles and then motorcars and running the company through its prosperous rise during the 1930s. Building was commenced on a new plant situated near Munich's Oberwiesenfeld airport, and Rapp Flugzeugwerke was amalgamated with several other local engine manufacturers in March 1917 to form Bayerische Motoren Werke: BMW.

Nevertheless, the firm was far from sound. It was not until 1917 that Popp and his engineer, Max Friz, were able to convince the German government to buy and fully support their own design engine, the BMW IIIa. The engine was a high-altitude powerplant of superb performance which was an immediate success, making the firm's fortune to the point that by mid-1918 BMW was licensing out production of the engine to a range of other manufacturers and was already producing a range of new designs. In August 1918 the company went public in excellent financial shape. By October 1918 it had 3500 employees, new plant, new designs and a wonderful future ahead of it as long as the war lasted.

The end of the war brought nationwide economic crisis and the collapse of government contracts, as well as intensive political instability. Throughout Germany the massive investment of the war years now took the form of unusable and idle excess productive capacity. Even worse for BMW, the Allies prohibited the production of any aircraft or aircraft engines by German manufacturers. BMW did not even have a product now. Popp and Friz tried many things, putting their productive capabilities into the manufacturer of farm machinery, marine engines, and truck engines. They even carried out illegal aircraft design, managing in conditions of absolute secrecy to break the world altitude record in 1919. As a result of this escapade, the authorities allowed the firm to attempt further records, but unfortunately would not give a green light to go back into production.

The firm was finally saved by a contract secured by Popp for the production of 10,000 railroad braking systems for Knorr-Bremse AG. Castiglioni read this as a signal to clear out of BMW while he had the chance, and sold his interest to Knorr-Bremse's chief stockholder. The latter wanted to turn BMW into a full-time brake-producing subsidiary, a prospect which left Popp less than enthusiastic and would have resulted in a very different history for the company.

Castiglioni, however, returned to save the day. In 1922 he bought back from Knorr-Bremse the BMW name, all its designs and some of the BMW plant. Moreover, he managed to buy the stock in the enormously devalued German currency of the inflationary period. With a cut-price company and the best engineering talent of the old firm still intact, the resurrected BMW immediately launched into the production of motorcycle engines. The BMW staff had seen the potential of this product right after the war and had developed the appropriate design already: this was the Bayern Kleinmotor.

Opposite page, top: Mechanics at work constructing aircraft engines in the Rapp Flugzeugwerke in 1917.

Opposite page, bottom: Company notables commemorating the production of their 500th engine.

Left and below: By 1922 BMW was producing motorcycles and motorcycle engines, beginning with the R32 (left). Motorcycle and aircraft engine production went on side by side. As the picture below shows, the motorcycle works was separated by a wooden fence from the aircraft division.

While initially relying on its truck motor sales for income, the success of the Kleinmotor rapidly convinced BMW to move into producing its own motorcycle, first with a design produced under license, then with its own BMW R32.

Throughout this period BMW was rapidly building up a great reputation and enormous sales. The demand for engines for both motorcycles and small cars was large and growing. In addition, in 1922 the prohibition on the German aircraft

industry was lifted and, by early 1923, BMW was back to its original forte. However, although it supplied engines to the wide range of small car manufacturers, the company had not yet taken the logical next step of producing its own car in order to complete its line.

As early as 1921, Castiglioni (not a stockholder at the time) came to the company with the prospect of producing a small sports car designed by Ferdinand Porsche, the 'Sascha.' This fell through, however, the circumstances not yet being right. The next step was protracted discussion from 1925 to 1928 of a car designed by Wunibald Kamm, which ended with no result. Nor could any support be found on the board of directors for BMW to design its own car. In fact the idea of going into cars, however obvious now, or technically logical then, still involved huge risk. The German automobile industry was in permanent crisis, as was still the economy, and many a small manufacturer was tottering on the brink. In addition, several other automotive interests were present on the BMW board and they would of course brook no BMW production which would compete with their share of the market.

It was therefore something of a masterstroke for Castiglioni to put forward Dixi-Werke as the best possible acquisition for BMW (with the eventual support of Jakob Schapiro, who was simultaneously major stockholder in Dixi and on the board of

Three views of the Dixi DA-1 in different body styles. The one on the right was a limousine version. Note the car in the top picture still bears the Dixi mascot.

Right: A Dixi DA-2.

Below: A 3/20hp limousine, BMW's first departure from their Austin Seven design. As the sign in the window indicates, this car had just won a race in Baden-Baden, 1932.

Opposite page: A Dixi van.

BMW). Dixi was a small company with — at long last — a bright future in the form of a great car to dominate the new small car market. From Dixi's side, it would need more capital to grow and would therefore benefit from the connection with a larger firm, while BMW's technical expertise matched its needs well. The Austin Dixi was after all only a small step up from motorcycles. The deal went through quickly and by 1 October 1928, Fahrzeugfabrik Eisenach (the Dixi-Werke) was a subsidiary of

BMW and the popular new Dixi 3/15 changed its name to the BMW 3/15hp.

Again, the logic was impeccable on both sides, but the deal was far from unproblematic: at the time of completion, for all its good reputation and rosy future, Dixi Werke had debts of RM11,000,000 to be set against total assets with a book value of RM4,996,487. Thus while BMW's sales had been increasing rapidly (from RM9.6 million in 1926 to RM27.2 million

in 1928), in 1929 it was forced to cut its dividend offer in half (to seven percent) even though Eisenach sales brought its gross figure up to RM40 million. The weight of this debt was not easy to absorb and was made even more difficult by the onset of the great depression, which cut BMW sales back to 1927 levels and led to drastic layoffs (BMW was still paying off Dixi debts well into the 1930s). However, BMW was in a relatively good position to survive bad times: as in the past (and again in the later 1940s), its healthy motorcycle sales, which were generally given a boost by bad times, kept a steady cash-flow going; its aircraft engines managed uninterrupted production; and, above all, its newly acquired 3/15 was the perfect car to weather a depression. BMW could not have done better if it had planned it.

The Austin Seven had been a major breakthrough in automobile marketing and production. Like the Ford Model T, it represented a move to make automobiles into a mass-market, consumer-oriented commodity which was to be sold to the broad middle class to meet their practical needs as well as their status-seeking. The car was no longer to be a mere luxury plaything of the rich, but the affordable and even sensible acquisition of the well-to-do. This was even more of a breakthrough for Austin and BMW than for an American manufacturer. The Europeans were far more — and for much longer — obsessed by a vision of the car as an expensive and highly customized item of conspicuous prestige consumption, closer to a work of craftsmanship than mass production — and this despite the massive sums of money they were investing (and often losing) in expensive production technology. Austin's slogan was 'Motoring for the Millions' and it was this winning strategy which BMW was cashing-in on with a very small, reliable, inexpensive car that could do equal

service for commuters, doctors, housewives, commercial travelers, families, and those who simply wanted a sample of that great symbol of modernity within their grasp. For them, the BMW 3/15 was not a lot more expensive than a motorcycle and sidecar, but a very different animal altogether.

As its name was meant to indicate, the 3/15 had three gears and an output of 15hp from a 747cc engine. The first model, the DA-1, was the Austin Seven without any modification. It cost RM2750 basic (compared to the Dixi 6/24, produced from 1924–28, and selling at RM6800 as a basic touring car). It was offered as a roadster, tourer, coupé and sedan. As everywhere the Austin appeared, the BMW 3/15 got rave reviews and top sales from the day it was introduced. The volume of production speaks for itself; a total of 25,000 3/15s were produced between 1927 and 1931. (This also included, incidentally, military purchases by the Reichswehr, which was at this time prohibited from purchasing heavy military vehicles and therefore bought and adapted 3/15s for maneuvers.)

BMW wisely refrained from altering or augmenting its little winner until 1929, when it was introduced in a DA-2 version with modifications inside and out: in particular with larger doors, an altered radiator and the outstanding innovation of four-wheel mechanical brakes. Its price ran from RM2200 for the two-seater sports car, through open four-seater, two-door sedan and cabriolet to convertible saloon at RM2625. A custom-built four-seater cabriolet at RM3200 was available to those wanting to indulge their old-style taste for exclusivity at a budget price. The DA-2 was followed by another very popular version, the DA-3, or Wartburg Sport, a minute two-seater sportster which could achieve 18hp and a very fast 53 mph (84 km/h). Selling for RM3100, it again got rave reviews and appeared prominently in the racing history of BMW.

The last BMW Austin model, the DA-4, introduced in 1932, marked a return to the original idea of the series. It was a very small but roomy-feeling, inexpensive and economical-to-run family car, beautifully engineered with advanced four-wheel brakes, simulated leather interior, excellent visibility and great reliability. Nonetheless, it did have its problems: Eisenach's ambitious engineers overreached themselves again by trying to improve upon the standard rigid front axle. Their resulting swing-axle suspension system generated steering and cornering problems and led to many complaints.

However well the BMW range did relatively, these were still bad years. Though BMW increased sales far more than the industry average, from as early as 1929 it had to introduce monthly instalment payments and accept increasing numbers of unsaleable old cars in part exchange. It also had great

difficulty in developing a dealership network at the bottom of the market; for Eisenach, which of course had been selling low-volume production models until now, this problem had not arisen. But the mass-volume 3/15 needed extensive sales backup, which BMW tried to provide by extending its motor-cycle sales network.

However, with the little Austin, BMW and the factory at Eisenach were able to ride out the storm and emerge into the mid-1930 in a strong position. It was to be an illustrious decade for them.

The Dixi DA-3, Wartburg Sport, was a popular and successful sports car, though it had a relatively short production run, with 400 units produced. As the top photograph, of a Wartburg Sport racing at St Moritz, illustrates, women racing car drivers were not an unusual sight in the 1920s and 1930s.

CHAPTER 3

THE CLASSIC YEARS

By the early 1930s, BMW had an established market position as a small-car manufacturer. It was fifth in total German car sales with a market share of 5.8 percent, behind Opel, a conglomerate called Auto Union, Daimler-Benz, and Adler. However it was not until 1932 that BMW began to break away from its Austin Dixi winner, and even then it was at first a careful evolution. In that year BMW canceled its Austin contract only weeks before it introduced the new car it had kept up its sleeve. It was the 3/20 AM-1.

The AM-1 had a redesigned engine of 785cc displacement with overhead valves producing 20hp and a top speed of 50 mph (80 km/h). The frame had also been completely redesigned into a new configuration – a central spine with swing axles. The swing wheel axles were improved over their DA-4 predecessors with transverse leaf spring; the same system was adopted for the back axles, but these were still far from a strong point. The AM-1 represented the beginning of BMW's break with small cars, being roomier and designed for long-distance comfort rather than simply getting about town. In styling, too, it could be considered attractive rather than cute, and with the feel of a larger car. The AM-1 was a heavy car and came in several body forms: four-seater roll-top sedan, carbriolet, and two-seater sports car. The car

achieved a production run of 7215 cars, not in the range of the popular 3/15, but respectable and keeping to a reasonable price of RM2650. But it was still very much a depression car, although BMW continued the series until 1934, making various modifications (particularly in the gearbox) to progress to an AM-4 model.

However in 1933 BMW brought out its first completely original design and began the run of prewar classic cars on whose reputation the company was able to survive through the long dark period until its next good run in the 1960s. The production runs on these cars were far from long even by the standards of those days, and the prices bounded rapidly upward as the decade progressed and the BMW engineers returned to their enthusiasm for big engines and high-performance cars. However it must be remembered that while the rest of the western world was mired in depression, for Germany the 1930s were a relative boom-time. Inflation was controlled, unemployment reduced, and production was rapidly expanding through a combination of political repression, default in reparations payments, and geared-up government spending on public works and military equipment. Thus, unlike the conditions obtaining during BMW's and Eisenach's other more unsuccessful periods of luxury car production during the 1920s and 1950s, Germany in the

1930s had a large and growing middle class, which was always BMW's real home market – the people it felt comfortable building cars for. This was also the age of Autobahn building (part of Hitler's public works program), which actually required the kind of car BMW was best at building. But it should also be borne in mind that, increasingly from the mid-1930s, BMW's real money – which allowed its low-volume automotive activities to continue – came from producing aircraft engines for the Luftwaffe (in fact, the Munich facilities were entirely devoted to aircraft production, all the cars being produced in Eisenach).

The 1933 model was the BMW 303, the first of its six-

Left and top: The sleek and stylized lines of the AM-4 mark the beginnings of BMW's age of classic designs.

Above: The AM-1 introduced an entirely new structure built along a central spine.

Right: A BMW 303 with unusual louvers and a flag that serves to recall the political loyalties of the class for which BMW was now producing.

Opposite page: A 303 juxtaposed with a modern 730 in front of the BMW museum in Munich.

Below: A well-preserved 303.

cylinder cars. The engine was in fact a six-cylinder version of the AM-4's four-cylinder, with 1175cc displacement, twin carburetors and an output of 30hp. The body was all new: available as two-door sedan, cabriolet, cabriosedan, and two-seater sports car, the 303 had clean, uncluttered and elegant lines with slanting side louvers and a long hood. The powerful motor and the car's sporty comfort and roomy interior justified its advertising claim to be the 'smallest big car in the world.' The body was mounted on a newly designed tubular frame, which BMW was to use well into the future, and included such innovations as folding front seats allowing for easy access to the back. The 303 had both the power and the comfort required for long-distance driving, all packed into a medium-sized car.

With the 303, BMW also introduced a stylistic feature which has been incorporated into every BMW produced since 1933: the BMW 'Nieren,' 'kidneys,' or twin-nose radiator grille. This feature has appeared in many different shapes and sizes since the 303, but has always remained a BMW identifying mark.

The 303 was the beginning of a long line of developments for BMW, both engine and body affording opportunities for many different variations. Not just from BMW: H J Aldington of Frazer Nash watched the 303 at the 1934 Alpine Trials. He was tremendously impressed by the car's performance, and particularly by the 303's now superb front suspension system. With the addition of new locating elements, the unsatisfactory AM-4 system had evolved into a modern unequal A-arm system. By 1935, Aldington had negotiated a license with Popp of BMW. Throughout the 1930s, BMWs arrived in the UK — most of them already fully assembled and undergoing only slight identification changes to become 'Frazer Nash-BMWs.' BMW 303 derivatives were produced in the UK well into the 1950s, under the names of Frazer Nash, Bristol and AC. The Frazer Nash connection also kept these cars prominent in the world of international racing, which was always a central publicity tool for BMW.

BMW started off its line of 303 derivatives in two opposite but equally logical directions with two cars introduced in 1934. Firstly, with the 309, it brought its four-cylinder line up to the new standard set by the 303. The 309 was identical to the 303 in its body and tubular frame but it carried an enlarged AM-4 engine and sold at RM400 below the price of the equivalent 303. In the other direction, BMW brought out the same 303 body with only minor modifications and an engine with expanded displacement: this was the 315 with a 1500cc engine and 34hp output. The next year it brought out an even more powerful version, the 319, with 45hp and a top speed of 71 mph (114 km/h). Both cars were very good sellers indeed (9215 and 6543 cars respectively) and consolidated BMW's position at the top end of the market, opposite Mercedes – its long-time rivals-to-be – but with a distinctively sporting bent. The 315 and 319 ultimately developed into a small production run of two-seater sports roadster versions, the 315/1 and 319/1, equipped with special 'sportsmotors' whose higher compression and three Solex carburetors brought the cars' hp to 40 and 55 respectively. These were very exclusive cars indeed, purely for the racer and very wealthy enthusiast, selling for over RM5000 (the basic 303 sedan cost only RM3600) and only 242

Top: A 315 adapted for the Reichswehr.

Right: A very beautiful 315/1 Roadster, a pinacle of BMW design and performance in the 1930s.

Top right: A 319 competing in the Nurburgring in 1979.

315/1s and 102 319/1s were produced.

However, the ultimate development of the overall sporty 303 chain of thought was one of the classic cars of the 1930s, the car which for the motor enthusiast stands out not only among BMWs but all prewar cars: the BMW 328. Looking from the outside like a comfortable roadster, and built on the same dimension wheelbase and tubular frame as the 315 and 319, it was a real powerhouse of a racing car. In fact, its first public appearance was at the Eifelrennen race on 14 July 1936, where it won first place with an average speed of 62.9 mph (101.3 km/h). It was a superbly streamlined car with gracefully curving front and rear end, headlights inserted in the front fenders, minimal running board and no side windows — in a word, no external obstructions to break its gentle but dynamic lines.

The BMW 328 was the company's true prewar classic car. It was both beautifully designed and dominated the race track throughout the late 1930s and even during the immediate postwar years in Europe.

In the best tradition of BMW it was elegant but with no frills. With the excellent suspension system of the 315, a light body and four-wheel hydraulic brakes, it had excellent handling, while its six-cylinder engine was completely re-designed to give a massive 80hp and a top speed of 93 mph

From the mid-1930s Frazer Nash built BMW cars for the British market, making virtually no changes on the German cars as can be seen from the 1939 Frazer Nash BMW 328 pictured on these pages.

Above: The aerodynamically designed 328 Mille Miglia.

Below: The big and expensive 326, here in cabriolet form, was BMW's flagship model, in the late 1930s.

Above: The 321, derived from the 326.

(150 km/h) and 110 mph (177 km/h) in its racing version. The 2-liter engine had a newly designed aluminum cylinder head, revolutionary camshaft system and three Solex downdraft carburetors. Its illustrious racing history will be taken up in a later chapter but, as a piece of classic automobile design, it was more than just a supercharged race winner. Predictably the car cost a small fortune at RM7400 and only 461 were produced, which only serves to make it the more coveted today as a vintage car.

Yet it was BMW's next model, still more expensive, which proved to be its most successful car of the decade. The 326 cost RM5500 but was in every respect one of the most advanced cars available. It ultimately sold (with its variations, the 320 and 321) over 15,000 cars. The 326 was another break in BMW's marketing policy and began a very different line of cars from those derived from the 303. An unquestionably *big* car, with a wheelbase of 113 inches compared to 94.5 for the 303-derived models, plus wider and roomier interior with more leg room, it was designed for relaxed and uncramped long-distance touring rather than for sprightly dashing about. The car underlined in all its details its substance and familial solidity: it had none of the sporty feel of the typical BMW but, rather, topped off the BMW range with a car to match the new confidence and stability of the emergent Fascist era. To underline its new role, the 326 was designed for a smooth ride: a deep-section box frame replaced the usual BMW tubular frame and was equipped with rack-and-pinion steering and a real innovation in the form of four-wheel hydraulic brakes. Moreover, the car had an all-new front and rear suspension system and a lateral locating bar to increase lateral stability. The all-steel body, produced by Ambi-Budd, was light for its size and very streamlined, with a spacious and well-appointed interior that could easily accommodate five people over long distances. Again backing up its touring role, the car was equipped with a fuel tank whose capacity allowed for 310 miles (500 km) with careful driving. The engine was close to that of the 315, with a displacement of 1900cc, overhead valves, and twin carburetors, all adding up to 50hp and a high top speed of 71 mph (114 km/h). The car was offered as a four-door sedan and two- or four-door cabriolet.

When it appeared, in 1936, the 326 was definitely a top-of-the-line automobile – right down to its eight-day clock – and was certainly the most praised car of that year.

BMW produced 326-type models right through the beginning of the war – in fact until 1941, when car production was brought to a halt. First came a transitional model: the 329, introduced in late 1936, was a 326 cabriolet body on a 319's tubular frame, with the old suspension and brake systems and an older motor. It was built for only one year, until the 319 was phased out, and consequently its frame and the 329 went too. There followed a model 320, a shorter and slightly cheaper version of the 326. The 320 continued to use the 319's suspension system and engine. This was succeeded in 1938 by the 321. In two-door sedan and cabriolet forms it was again identical to, but shorter than, the 326, but this time with the latter's advanced engineering included. The 321's only other claim to fame is that it served as the point of departure for the postwar production of BMW's East German successor, EMW, continuing production until 1955.

The final development of the 326 big six-cylinder line was the 335, which made its appearance in 1939. This was an even larger version of the 326, a really big car with a wheelbase of 117.5 inches, built as a four-door sedan and two- and four-door cabriolet. It had a huge 3.5-liter, six-cylinder engine which gave out 90hp and could be pushed to 90 mph (150 km/h). With its big engine and comfortable interior, it was once again a long-distance cruiser for the upper middle-class and BMW's most direct challenge yet to Mercedes. However, it was already the 11th hour: war was underway by the time 335 production had begun, materials became unobtainable or irregular in supply, and production facilities went over to military manufacture. BMW managed only 410

units of the 335 before production of civilian vehicles came to a halt in 1941.

However, there was one other derivative of the 326, and this one was another classic car. The 327, introduced in 1937, was a sporty version of the 326, but retained the latter's long-distance comfort. It had the 320's shorter wheelbase, but the 326's suspension system and a two-liter engine with 55hp. Originally presented as a two-seater cabriolet and then as a two-seater coupé, it was gorgeously sleek with an outrageously sloping and drawn-out rear end – a very elegant car indeed. In 1939, it also appeared as a 327/28, a 327 with an 80hp engine capable of 87mph (140 km/h) and costing

Far left, left, and below: The 335 was the ultimate development of BMW's big six-cylinder cars, produced from 1939–41. It was BMW's largest model yet, and met with considerable demand despite the outbreak of war and shortage of materials.

Opposite page, bottom: The 325 was built from 1937–40 under contract to the Reichswehr, a heavy-duty, jeep-like construction.

in the region of RM8000.

BMW finished the decade and entered the war having managed to achieve huge and rapid growth: from 1928 sales of RM27,000,000 and employment of 2630 workers, it finished 1939 with gross sales of RM275,000,000 and 26,919 employees. Again, much of this growth came from BMW's aircraft engine division, which expanded along with German rearmament. Even the automotive section shared in the money-flow from military growth: from 1937 to 1940, BMW manufactured 3225 units of the 325. This was a car designed under contract to the Wehrmacht and emerged as a huge and heavy military vehicle, a jeep-like affair with structural reinforcement, four-wheel drive and equipped with tires for off-road driving. The BMW emblem was discreetly left off.

From the outbreak of war in September 1939 until 1941, BMW was able to continue producing cars, though fitfully for the most part. From the start the government placed heavy, sometimes total, restrictions on the production of private passenger cars. BMW managed at first to obtain partial exemptions from these regulations. However supplies — particularly of tires — were rapidly exhausted and could only be obtained through the government as part of contracts for the High Command. Ironically, however, there was still very strong private demand for cars throughout the early years of the war, with dealers screaming for more cars to sell. The Germans started the war with enormous confidence, believing they were strong enough to fight a world war while carrying on normal business and private life at the same time.

However, this was wartime, after all, and after May 1941 Eisenach was completely turned over to war production, including military motorcycles. It survived the war with very little damage. The Munich plant, on the other hand, gradually moved its operations out into the countryside, but was very heavily bombed. Though BMW's normal activity was disrupted, under 1942 war production conditions their gross earnings were RM561,000,000 (double that of 1939) and they employed 47,346 people (though it is not certain if this includes Jews and other prisoners from Dachau employed under conditions of forced labor). War is good for business — but only until bombing and defeat disrupt production. As we shall see in the next chapter, despite the company's glorious decade of growth in the 1930s, there was absolutely nothing left of BMW in 1945 and, except for the continuity of some of the top management and engineering staff, the company which emerged after the war was virtually all new.

Left and above: The 327 combined the size and comfort of the 326-derived models with a sportier feel and a very powerful motor (it was available with a 328 engine). Note that one car has front-opening doors, the other rear-openers: many of the big BMWs followed an inconsistent policy on this design feature.

CHAPTER 4

RISING FROM THE ASHES

The postwar story of BMW is one of an immensely long and hard struggle to emerge from the ashes after the war. It was unable to begin producing cars again until 1951, always found itself one step behind Mercedes throughout the 1950s, and was very near bankruptcy by 1959. It was only saved by its good reputation (though this was wearing thin with the banks) and by the popular success of one of its most un-BMW-like products to date. Despite some fine design work during these years – in fact partly because of it – BMW was still convalescent until the early 1960s and the patient almost died.

In 1945, BMW was left with absolutely nothing. The Eisenach factory happened to end up eight kilometers inside the Russian sector and so BMW lost its entire automobile-producing plant to East Germany. The factory was nationalized to become the Eisenach Motoren Werke (EMW) and until 1955 produced copies of prewar BMW models, in particular the 321, for export. In 1955 however it ran into problems of unfair competition in its use of the BMW name in Western Europe.

As for BMW's Munich premises, most of it had been bombed well into the ground. Much of what was left was dismantled and shipped out by the Allies as reparations: BMW had, after all, been a major producer of military engines during the war. The USA took over the relatively intact Allach works to carry out their own army vehicle repairs, eventually paying rent to BMW. Dismantling of other BMW plant stopped short of complete razing.

The slow process of resurrection began in 1945. As in 1919, the company tried to produce whatever it could, in this case pots and pans, bicycles, some farm machinery, and brake compressors. Up until 1948, BMW was not allowed to produce *any* vehicles, even motorcycles, and even after 1948 only cycles of under 250cc capacity. These it then built, in the form of the R24, and, in the context of an austerity-driven boom in motorcycle sales – the only vehicle that people could in any case afford – it laid the foundations of its revival. By 1953, BMW was producing 100,000 motorcycles, many of them for export.

But still no cars – or at least no BMW cars produced by BMW; instead there were only the EMW models for distribution on the continent. In Britain, H J Aldington of Frazer Nash wanted to build on his company's profitable prewar relation-ship with BMW and attempted to import the whole BMW design team to England as a brains trust, but he failed to extract the necessary work permits from his government. Instead he set up production of BMW's classic prewar 328 sports car model, using the now excess capacity of the Bristol Aeroplane Company, and sold it as the Bristol 400. A number of BMW designers, under Ernst Loof, set up a company called Veritas which produced racing-cars based on BMW designs. They had limited success and lasted until 1950.

BMW's return to car production was dictated by available resources; it simply did not have the finances to set up elaborate production facilities. Thus coachwork was contracted out until the middle 1950s and engines were based on what could be made from equipment which had survived the war. However, BMW compounded its problems and from the beginning laid the basis of its continuous instability throughout the decade. It resurrected the marketing philosophy which had brought it close to ruin after the First World War and which had only worked in the very different circumstances of the 1930s: returning to production much later than most auto-motive firms, BMW encountered a market already crowded with small cars and therefore decided to launch with an expensive, small-volume product. Hence it found itself nose-to-nose with only one major competitor, but one which it could not hope to displace: Mercedes. Moreover, the luxury market which Mercedes dominated was in any case extremely small in those days of German weakness and would remain so for some time as the German 'Economic Miracle' slowly gathered momentum. Nonetheless BMW continued to produce for a market which hardly yet existed, letting the BMW engineers pursue their mania for very large, very expensive and very high-powered six-cylinder, then V8, monsters – among the fastest cars on the German roads.

In any event, BMW made its return to the automobile world at the 1951 Frankfurt show with its 501. It attracted a lot of attention, received good press reports and considerable advanced orders. Unfortunately it also took BMW a full year to gear up for production and start filling those orders. The 501 was very closely based on the prewar best-seller, the 326. It used the same six-cylinder 1979cc engine, but with its efficiency increased to produce 65hp and a speed of 84 mph (135 km/h). The car included some very advanced structural work, mounted on a combined box-section frame and tubular chassis with an all-new suspension system, the old transverse leafs giving way to a torsion-bar system. The body was cer-tainly substantial, if a bit lumpy from the outside, and was dubbed the 'Baroque Angel' in allusion to its rather over-flowing curves, though its swooping fender lines and taste-fully minimal use of chrome did make for elegance, and its absence of running boards made for both cleaner lines and wider interior. Inside it was quite roomy and incorporated some now-popular American features, such as steering-column-mounted gear shift, but its instrument panel was identical to the old 326.

Despite a warm reception, BMW's 501 was in direct com-petition with Mercedes, whose comparable models were cheaper (BMW's low-volume production precluded lower prices to begin with), more powerful and more attractive. Furthermore, BMW had problems with distribution, with hardly any dealership network of its own and other dealers already preoccupied with selling Mercedes in the same price

Above: Before BMW got back into production after the war, many derivatives of its cars were built by other companies. This one is a postwar Bristol.

bracket. Finally, BMW had no real exports, nor much chance of obtaining them (exports were achieved in the mid-1960s when it had a very different kind of car). Again, much like other periods in its history, BMW was sustained by its still very healthy motorcycle sales.

BMW quickly followed up with the 501A, a version both cheaper and more highly powered, and, later in the same year (1952), with a stripped-down version with only basic equipment that was cheaper still: DM12,500 as opposed to DM15,150 for the original 501. However, BMW produced a total of only 6328 501s in its three versions during its production life from 1952 to 1955. The next version was BMW's last six-cylinder for a while: the 501/3 was the basic 501 with its engine bored-out to give a 2077cc displacement and an output of 72hp.

BMW's next advance, which was to be its basic line of development throughout the rest of the decade, was its introduction of the 502 in 1954. Set in the same 501 body, it housed Germany's first postwar V8 engine. This 2580cc, 100hp monster was not only an exclusive selling point but something of a technical necessity for powering the huge car. It was also the first engine with aluminum heads and block. Despite its price of DM17,800, the 502 V8 was BMW's best-

Top and above: The 502 V8 Cabrio was the first postwar German car to carry a V8 engine.

selling car of the 1950s, with a run of 5955 cars. Virtually indistinguishable from the 501, until the addition of wraparound rear windows in 1955, it had a very plush interior.

BMW issued several V8 variations over the next few years.

mostly containing only engine changes. The 501 V8 of 1955 was simply the 502 without trimmings and was later called the 2.6. In 1955, the company introduced the 3.2, which was simply the same V8 again, bored out to give a 3168cc engine with 120hp and 105 mph (169 km/h). However, from 1958 it also came with power steering and – a year later – front disc brakes, well before they were available on other models. This car, with yet more power, became available as the 3.2 Super in 1957 and was noted for its distinctive whistle at high speeds. The 2.6 became the 2600 when it was

given a faster engine in 1961. In the same year, BMW came out with the logical extreme in this range of cars with the 3200: the last of the BMW V8s, it was capable of 0–60 mph

Right and below: BMW adhered to one unchanging model throughout the 1950s for its top-of-the-line car: this was the 502 'Baroque Angel' and was as globular and pretentious as much 1950s design.

(0–97 km/h) in 13.5 seconds and a top speed of 109 mph (175 km/h) and 118 mph (190 km/h) in its 3200S version. It was for a while the fastest private car on the German roads.

The proliferation of model numbers notwithstanding, and despite the variations BMW played on its engines, the company stuck to the same basic car with perverse doggedness during the decade. It did not change its styling in the least and was virtually selling one type of car throughout the 1950s: the last V8 sedan to roll off the assembly line in 1964 looked just like the first, only now it was rather anachronistic. Nor did it produce a cheaper but related car which might have acted to support its fleet leader with some volume sales. In fact, by 1964 BMW had sold 9973 six-cylinder cars and 12,777 V8s. This was a reasonable success given the prevailing conditions, but far from what was necessary to recreate a motoring giant.

Seeing that something was definitely wrong and that some sort of breakthrough was needed, BMW charged off in two completely different directions, encountering two quite different forms of failure at opposite ends of the market. At the 1955 Frankfurt show, BMW simultaneously introduced three of its most exclusive luxury cars ever, and one of the cheapest cars ever produced.

First came the luxury cars, all three of which received outstanding critical acclaim. One was the 505, which never saw production, being limited to two prototypes, The 505 was a limousine designed to be an inordinately prestigious car of state. More important were two designs by Albrecht Goertz, both derived from the basic 501 sedan, but with a real difference. First was the 503. Conceived as a sporty version of the 501 and available as cabriolet coupé, it was a high-speed V8 touring car, though not very roomy. The engine revved up a massive 140hp for a top speed of 118 mph (190 km/h) with the car's light-weight construction. With all this, plus a lavish interior, the 503 sold at *double* the price of the 501 and, not surprisingly, for all its beauty of line and performance, only 412 were sold.

The second Goertz' design and the third BMW car un-

veiled at the 1955 show was a true sports car, and BMW's first postwar classic, the 507. A two-seater with a V8 engine, capable of 120 mph (193 km/h), it had superb performance and the cleanest, most subtle line available, its arrow-head front end especially pointing to the shape of things to come. However, like the 503, it was a very expensive car indeed (DM26,500) — a feat of engineering and design over marketing. BMW was still selling exclusivity, to its own detriment; production lasted only until 1960, with a total of a mere 253 cars produced.

Away at the other end of the market, at the same 1955 show, BMW introduced a car so cheap and plain that, after seven years of production and huge sales, most people to this day do not associate it with the name of BMW. The car was the Isetta, designed by an Italian motorcycle manufacture named Renzo Revolta. The 'mini-est' car ever mass produced, it had a

The Touring 503, above, and the 507 sports car, right, were BMW's only design departures from the 501/502 during the 1950s, and they were attractive cars.

two-stroke 250cc motorcycle engine. It started life as a three-wheeler but, even with the later addition of a second back wheel, the wheels were so close together they looked like only one. The most distinctive feature of the car was its one door: the whole front end of the car, steering column, pedals and all, opened up for access and egress. Like the VW Beetle, the

The 507, seen here in cut-away and fully clothed, was a superbly designed V8 sports car capable of 150hp. It also had a detachable hard-top, not shown here.

Isetta was an endearingly ugly car — soon dubbed the 'rolling egg' — which carried economy and lack of style to the point where it became a positive virtue — for a while. It was a real no-frills city car, designed simply to be physically capable of getting a driver, plus one cramped passenger, around town.

BMW obtained a license from Revolta's Iso SpA of Milan, substituted their own 247cc motorcycle engine, and began production in 1955, selling their Isetta 250 for DM2580. In 1957 this model was discontinued, having been replaced in 1956 by a second body type and a 297cc engine. By the end of its life in 1962, BMW had produced 162,000 Isettas. Even more were made in England under license from BMW.

BMW soon began making improvements in the Isetta, but these were directed more by engineering concerns than by any concerted marketing strategy. In 1957, BMW intro-

Opposite top: Cut-away diagram of the 600, when the Isetta was already evolving into a car, with nearly normal back wheels.

Opposite below: This wedding photograph captures some of the bizarre appeal of the rolling egg.

Left: Does this look like a BMW to you?

duced the 600, in which the frame of the Isetta was altered so that the rear wheels had the same distance from each other as the front ones; it now had one side door, in addition to the front opening, leading to a back seat for two. It also had a revolutionary rear suspension system which BMW used on all cars thereafter (and which was adopted by Rolls-Royce, Mercedes, and GM). However well crafted, the 600 still looked like the Isetta: the excellent design was hidden behind the bottom-of-the-market image of the car. Sales were disappointing (34,318 between 1957 and 1959), and covered very little of the shortfall left by declining sedan sales.

The Isetta made sense for BMW as a motorcycle manufacturer of note: it used BMW's expertise in this area, as well as its motorcycle-engine producing capacity. More importantly, however, as indicated earlier, with its high price, low-turnover product at the top end of the car market, BMW was heavily dependent on its motorcycle sales to finance its automobile output. Yet by the mid-1950s even this consolation was leaving the company. The motorcycle market was approaching crisis (BMW sold 29,699 motorbikes in 1954, only 5400 in 1957) and BMW sales were in jeopardy from its most reliable revenue source. Peope were moving up into prosperity and therefore cars, and BMW had to move with them. The Isetta was that one step up. However, despite huge sales, the Isetta — as well as the 600 and the later 700 — had profit margins which were far too low, a precarious market position and no relation whatsoever to the rest of BMW's product range. It could not seriously remain the dependent high-volume foundation for BMW's continued stability or growth as a car manufacturer.

By this point in the late 1950s, BMW was reaching a desperate financial situation. Although it now knew what it needed to do — produce a middle-range car — it could not raise the finance to do it. Another stopgap was being developed and was finally introduced in 1959: this was the BMW 700. Although it was another mini-car, based entirely on Isetta design in engineering terms, its body was designed by Michelotti of Turin and bore no resemblance whatsoever to an egg. It was sporty, but still a no-nonsense car without showy trimmings, a functional but relatively roomier family car in its sedan form and a good inexpensive sportster as a coupé. Engine size was increased from that of the 600 to a displacement of 697cc, yielding 30hp. The 700 was brought out in two further versions. The 700LS, introduced in 1962, had a longer wheelbase to give extra leg-room to the back passengers; this was done in order to give the car more conviction as a larger-than-playtoy vehicle, and more than a motorcycle with a roof. It came out first as a Luxus with special features, then in a standard version and later as a coupé. Finally, in 1960, the 700 Sport (later called the 700CS) was introduced, first as a coupé and then in a cabriolet version. It was built for (relative) speed and handling, with a 40hp engine and anti-roll bars, and had a surprising and successful career in racing and rallying.

The 700 was a last straw, gratefully grasped. It came out at a time when BMW was under very heavy pressure from its banks, had lost all direction and sense of the future, and was fighting off a series of takeover bids, culminating in a refinancing offer which involved an extremely unfavorable merger with Mercedes. This merger was actually to be announced as an accomplished fact at a stockholders' meeting on 9 December 1959. The deal was only averted by a rebellion among the smaller stockholders — led by an adept lawyer by the name of Friedrich Mathern — who wished to keep the company independent and believed in its future. After this, one of the major stockholders, Herbert Quandt, put his prestige, reputation, and influence behind independence; the entire management was restructured and new policies were evolved. At the same time, the 700, which had only been

Left: Closer view of the Isetta's strange means of access.

Below: It was the 700, here shown in later LS version, which gave BMW a new lease of life.

introduced in August, began to take off, and arguments for BMW's viability had more credibility.

The 700 was a reprieve, for it was the only thing that could keep BMW going long enough for it to try to get its marketing right. In fact, the 700 was an enormous success in sales terms — 188,000 of them in their several versions being sold from 1959 to 1965. Nor were they all that cheap, the 700 sedan selling at DM4760 and the 700 LS sedan at DM5850. But, despite such sales, a lot was packed into them and the profit margin for BMW on the 700 was very slim indeed. In any case, it was always more in the nature of an aberration in BMW's overall development: a lucky development of a very subsidiary product-line unrelated to the company's real area of expertise and image, it could be no more than a temporary stopgap, giving BMW the luxury of one last chance.

CHAPTER 5

THE 'NEW CLASS'

Over the next few years, BMW once again became a virtually new company, carrying over from its past little more than its reputation for great engineering and high prices for luxury cars. Yet it was now that BMW leapt from being a producer of thousands of cars to hundred of thousands of cars per year. When we think of BMW today, it is really the post-1961 BMW we are thinking of – a relatively recent company.

The success of the 700, coinciding with the appearance in 1960 of a good-selling new motorcycle – the R27 – saved the company from bankers and takeovers for the moment. More importantly, it laid the foundation, financially, for the company to gear itself up and finally get things right. There was now no reason for BMW not to put its superb engineering and more erratic design creativity into a well-built but affordable middle-class car which would make marketing sense and generate mass sales.

Despite a series of prototypes and certain technical and stylistic precedents (particularly in the 700 and the 3200CS designed by Bertone), the BMW 1500, which made its motor show debut in 1961, was a complete revolution in BMW design and was precisely what was called for. It was the first of what BMW called the 'New Class' cars and was indeed completely new from top to toe, inside and out.

Designed in-house, though with advice from Michelotti, it retained the general shape of the 700 but on a much larger scale and with more elegance and fine detail. A central change in the car was the addition of the older arrow-shaped front end, which removed the last of the bulbous-nose look and has been an integral part of all BMW styling since then. Using an all-welded, frameless construction, it was a clean-looking car, soft-spoken but with prestige and obvious technical sophistication. It used no chrome but, rather, molded contours to accentuate its lines, and it had lots of large windows to give it a light and airy look. In the style and mood that was to mark all BMW cars down to the present day, the 1500 was unpretentious, even practical, but without employing showy signals. To the discerning eye it was clearly a car of prestige, quality, and power.

Above right: The 2000 was introduced by BMW in 1966.

Below: Huge sales of the 700 coincided with the popularity of the R27 motorcycle, raising the cash which made the New Class cars possible.

Inside, the car was as roomy as the old 502 V8 (at half its price), its austere elegance reflected in its rather empty no-frills dashboard. The engine, too, was all-new, a quiet four-cylinder, five-bearing engine with overhead camshaft, generating 75hp, and promising plenty of opportunity for improvement. The car also incorporated BMW's unique semi-trailing-arm rear-suspension system. And this time, BMW kept to four-cylinders, leaving the bigger engines for later and marketing them as an identifiably separate line.

The 1500 immediately received good press reviews, placing it at the top of its class. It was a practical car, but with class, which finally combined BMW's still-respected name for top-quality engineering in luxury cars, with a product financially and functionally tailored to a now-expanding middle-class market. At a price of DM9485, the 1500 was definitely competitive. Moreover, it finally allowed BMW to withdraw from its hopeless contest with Mercedes into a substantial market which then contained *no* domestic competitors. Instead it contained many consumers, with money in their pockets, who were looking for an alternative to the available American models.

The readiness of the market was made obvious by its response to a problem that had dogged BMW throughout its history. Although the car was an immediate success, it was slow in getting into full-scale production. By the end of one full year's delay BMW had 20,000 firm orders to fill. But despite the delay, the orders kept coming. Once in production, BMW was rapidly operating at full capacity. During the 1500's lifetime, from October 1962 to December 1964, 23,807 of them were produced.

This short production run was partly due to an untypical problem for BMW. The basic idea of the 1500 was undoubtedly right but, for all intents and purposes BMW was once again a virtually new company. It had had to develop the car in a rush to make the most of the little breathing space it had. As a result, the 1500 had many serious technical faults, particularly with its axle and gearbox. Ironically, then, BMW's reputation for prestige engineering – the one quality which had kept the firm afloat – was in danger just when it had finally got its marketing and styling right.

Nonetheless, the 1500 was the beginning of a remarkable run of great cars, the series lasting until 1972 before any

major changes were again made. Until that date, BMW adhered to a disciplined strategy of maintaining one basic idea and working a large number of small variations on it. In this case, BMW consistently sold the same basic bodies – a four-door and later two-door sedan – with three different engines – 1600, 1800 and 2000cc plus variations of these. This made for a profusion of names but little fundamental change.

In 1963, BMW introduced its 1800, a 1500 body with a bigger engine (90hp) and with solutions to most of the technical faults of the 1500. At the same time, BMW showed yet another version, the 1800 TI: again, everything the same except for the two carburetors and a higher compression ratio for the engine, allowing for 110hp and 105 mph (170 km/h) top speed. BMW's marketing was based on its reputation for high-powered, top-performance cars after all and the company was careful to show souped-up versions alongside all new models. But even the simple 1800 showed the essence of BMW's offer to the public – a comfortable, practical, even family-type car in sedan shape, but with sports-car performance. Over 120,000 of these two 1800s were produced between 1963 and 1968.

In 1964, the first cycle of the New Class was completed with the 1600, identical again in body, detail and price to the 1500, but with none of its faults and closer to it in performance than the 1800. By now, BMW was firmly on its feet as a company and, though still quite small compared to the motoring giants, steadily growing and in excellent financial shape. Most importantly, it was now patently viable for the foreseeable future, with a basis laid for considerable expansion.

For its next set of developments, BMW concentrated on expanded power, introducing its two-liter engine in several different packages. First, in 1965, came BMW's first New Class coupé, the 2000 C/CS, capable of 120hp with its Solex carburetors, but heavy and with less than optimum sports-car performance. In 1966 the 2000 appeared in sedan versions. One could get the high-performance engine in a no-frills 1800 body at a low price, or in the 2000 tilux, which had the most luxurious interior ever offered by BMW's New Class. Finally, in 1969, came the ultimate development of the whole four-cylinder, four-door sedan range, the 2000 tii, carrying a fuel injection engine with an output of 130hp.

While BMW concentrated on these high-output cars, it also introduced, again in 1966, a more down-market model

Opposite page: The 1802, sitting between the 1602 and 2002 in engine capacity, was introduced later than the other two, in 1971. It was these two-door models which really brought BMW to prominence in the American market, which might have something to do with the setting of this photograph.

Above: The 2000 C had a two-door body quite different from the New Class cars, more closely related to the 3200 CS.

Left: The 2800 CS.

which yielded surprising results and developed into an enduring line. The 1600-2 was a two-door sedan version of the 1600, but lighter, shorter, narrower, lower, and less expensive, with superb performance to boot. This two-door car proved to be a breakthrough for BMW and in its 1600-2 and later 1602 version (renamed after a cosmetic retouching in 1971) sold 277,320 cars — more than the 1600 and 1800 four-doors combined. Above all, the 1600-2 marked BMW's serious entry into the American market. The combination of top-quality engineering and performance, packaged in clean lines with a functional lack of flashiness, was unlike anything

available in the USA and the motoring press went wild.

It was actually BMW's next step along this 1600-2 route which produced its authentic cult car of the 1960s and early 1970s. In 1967, it produced a Ti version of the 1600-2 — that

Left: A 1600 on the rally track. New Class cars did not have an illustrious racing history.

Below: A cabriolet version of the 2002, the body converted by Baur in 1971.

is to say, a version with identical engineering but with a souped-up 105hp twin-carburetor engine. Unfortunately, this car could not comply with the United States' stiff exhaust-emission laws. In order to increase the 1600-2's performance without exacerbating the exhaust problems BMW simply increased the engine's displacement, putting a 100hp, 2-liter engine into the 1600-2 body. The resulting car, the 2002, was an authentic wolf in sheep's clothing; fast, agile,

Far left: Testing engines in the BMW plant.

Left: Back view of the 2002 tii, a fuel-injected version of the already-powerful 2002ti.

Below: The Baur Cabriolet seen with its hard top on.

Right: The 2000 tii Touring, like BMW's other hatchbacks, was not a successful car, despite its powerful motor.

economical, with fantastic cornering, it was really a sports car with the extra bonus of roominess and family-style comfort. The 2002 was an even better seller than the 1600-2, both in the USA and Europe, with 398,434 produced (including the 2002 ti version and 2002 tii with fuel-injection engine) between 1968 and 1976, when it was the last of the New Class cars to be discontinued. To this day American 2002 drivers salute each other on the road.

BMW's final variations in this hugely successful run of four-cylinder cars were its Touring models, introduced in 1971. These were hatchbacks, produced in 1600, 1800, 2000 and 2000 tii (fuel injection) versions. The 2000 Touring models were the most successful, being one of the most powerful of this class of car on the market. But with sales of only 11,000, obviously even this had hardly taken hold. It simply did not represent what people wanted or expected from BMW.

As BMW became assured of the success of the 1500 in the early 1960s, and the development of its four-cylinder line was begun, the firm began to ease most of its earlier models off the assembly line. By 1965, all its Isettas, 600s and 700s, as well as its six-cylinder and V8 models at the upper end of the scale, were phased out of production. Its last big luxury car had been the 3200CS, produced from 1962 to 1965, costing DM29,850 (compared to DM9485 for the 1500, which was introduced simultaneously). A beautiful Bertone-designed sporting coupé with 160hp V8 engine, it had a production run of only 603. When, in 1968, BMW decided to have a go at big cars again, times had changed. Its 2500 model had both engine and styling closely and clearly based on its four-cylinder models. With its smooth running six-cylinder, 150hp engine and spacious interior, BMW had kept its winning logic of combining sportiness, practicality, and comfort. The same sedan was also offered in a more luxurious version with a 2800 engine, and together they sold 137,455 between 1968 and 1977. The 2800 turned out to be too expensive for the American market, so in 1971 BMW offered a neat compromise, introducing the Bavaria: this was the 2500 body with a 2800 engine and no frills. Offering outstanding performance and power at a budget price (for a luxury car) it was another BMW classic. There was also a 2800 CS sports coupé, introduced in 1968, basically a six-cylinder engine in the 2000 CS body.

Finally, in 1971, to top off their line, BMW began a line of three-liter cars starting with the 3.0 S, later known as the Bavaria. This was also offered with fuel-injected engine, the 3.0 Si. For an expensive car (DM19,980 for the 3.0 S at the time of its introduction) it was very popular and sold extremely well: 52,877 of the two models were produced. In the same year BMW also introduced the 3.0 CS, a coupé to follow the 2800 CS. In 1974 came the 3.3 L, whose body had a longer wheelbase than the other sixes, giving more leg room. To some extent, however, this car was a white elephant, coming onto the market in the middle of the oil crisis and the depth of the mid-1970s depression. It cost DM37,550 and only 3022 units

Far left: The Bavaria was one of BMW's biggest selling high-priced cars.

Left: The 2800 CS was basically a six-cylinder version of the 2000 CS, though with an improved front end. It was a very attractive car.

Below: The 3.0 L was a 3-liter development of the 2500/2800 series.

were produced. During 1974, even the very rich were taken with price panic.

Still at the upper end of power and price, BMW produced two turbo-charged models in the early 1970s. The first was strictly for show, a dream car which was limited to two proto-types representing the combined Utopian vision of the engineer and the stylist. It was developed to be unveiled at the 1972 Olympics which were held in BMW's home town of Munich. Called simply the Turbo, its turbocharged engine put out around 200hp from a four-cylinder, two-liter engine. However, the aim of the exercise was not simply to show that hair-raising speeds – in this case 155 mph (250 km/h) – could be coaxed out of a relatively small engine. The Turbo was also designed to show off the most advanced safety features available, including gimmicks such as radar which warned the driver if he was below the correct braking distance from the car ahead for a given speed. But other safety features were more impressive, particularly in the area of crash absorption. The Turbo had foam-filled front and rear panels, which passed impact on to telescoping steel beams, and had reinforced side-impact bars in its doors.

In 1973, BMW actually put a turbo-charged car into mass-production, the 2002 turbo (in fact *the* Turbo had been built on a 2002 chassis). Though fast and with all the advantages of the 2002's now-classic design and engineering, the 2002 turbo lasted only one year and 1672 units, being rather an anachronism in the middle of the oil crisis. In fact despite its basis in the 2002, much about the turbo version – it was very low to the ground, with wide wheels, a dashing front spoiler, and multicolored stripes down its sides – feels like a last gesture of the Swinging Sixties.

In fact, BMW had already sensed the changing times and acted accordingly, subtly adjusting only the edges of its cars' image in a direction that proved to be utterly appropriate to the more low-key, restrained and financially insecure 1970s. Moreover, the car that inaugurated this shift in 1972 became the core of an astonishingly integrated marketing policy which shrewdly, logically and economically covered all the options for car sizes and types within BMW's overall market area. For a now-huge corporation, it was to prove a period of remarkably adept consolidation of its gains.

Left: The 2002 turbo, though an obvious technical development of the two-door line, was inappropriate to the mid-1970s period of recession and inflation.

Above: The engine of the 2002 turbo.

Overleaf: The Turbo was a dream car of the future, but one based on sound and sensible research into safety.

This 1972 car, the 520, was BMW's first departure from the New Class series — as its new model designation system implied (the last two digits represent the deca-liter displacement of the engine). But there was a subtle departure: the look of the new four-door sedan, though less blocky, was almost identical to the older models, above all the 2000, although there was less stress on sports performance and engine power. BMW emphasized the comfort of the car — always an ingredient in the company's mix — with a longer wheelbase and more leg room. In fact, the 520 was closer in size to the six-cylinder models than to the 2000. The engine was a revamped four-cylinder two-liter, generating 115hp with two Stromberg CD downdraft carburetors. The chassis and all-independent suspension system were advances on the New Class models, but were not the crucial difference. Rather it was the family-oriented practicality of the car which marked the change to the new mood of the 1970s. The large number of safety features incorporated into the unibody structure also reflected new concerns. Many had been explored through the

development of the Turbo — especially the crash absorption measures to counter the effects of crash. These included an impact-absorbing front end and a reinforced 'safety cell' for the passenger area. The 520 also marked the beginning of a new line of advance in design with the introduction of ergonomically engineered dashboard and controls arrangements. This new stress on driver comfort and control were to be developed through the coming 3- and 6-Series into the concept of 'Cockpit Design.'

Several variants of the '5-Series' appeared during the 1970s, but all were identical to the 520 in body design. It was the engine that kept changing; a 520i was introduced simultaneously with the 520 — simply a fuel-injected version of the same engine. The 525 of 1973 carried a new six-cylinder 2.5-liter engine of 145hp capacity and in 1975 the same body housing a 2.8-liter, six-cylinder engine became the 528 (a further fuel-injected 528i superseded it in 1977). A 520-6,

Below: The 520 was BMW's first step into a new integrated line of cars for the 1970s.

Opposite page, left: Interior of the 520. The new series had more leg room than the old New Class.

Opposite page, right: Another early 5-Series car.

inaugurated in 1977, took over from the 520i. BMW also expanded into lesser-powered vehicles with the 518, an oil-crisis model introduced in 1974. This contained a 90hp, 1.8-liter, four-cylinder engine aimed at the European market. There was also a six-cylinder 5-Series car, the 530/530i, produced solely for the American market. This was the only 5-Series BMW to appear in the USA.

The 5-Series was an enormous success. Offering the usual BMW top-quality value for money at reasonably competitive prices, the total output of all the 5-Series from 1972 to 1978 was 467,112 cars. However, after the 520 was introduced in 1972, BMW waited to see how it would do, and gave it time to catch on, before phasing out the older New Class models (above all the two-door classics) and expanding the new line.

Nonetheless, in July 1975 came the new 3-Series. Aiming to replace gradually the old -02 series of two-door cars with vehicles more in line with the new thinking, the series began with the 316 and 318. The body was designed by Paul Bracq — designer of the Turbo — to be, like the 5-Series, longer, wider and more spacious than its predecessors. But as with all BMW two-door sedans, it had to retain the good handling of a sporty car. Thus it had a suspension system derived from the old 2500 line and also included rack-and-pinion steering, which BMW had not used since the 700/LS. The first two

models carried four-cylinder engines of 1.6-liter and 1.8-liter displacement respectively (90hp and 98hp). These engines, like the later 320, carried 2-barrel carburetors and a newly-designed combustion chamber. Being introduced in the middle of recession, they were designed to run on regular gasoline.

Again, the variations were solely in the engines. Later in 1975 came the four-cylinder 320 and fuel-injected 320i. The 320i, with Bosch-K Jetronic, was the only 3-Series car that could pass the strict test of US emissions laws. It achieved this through a combination of low compression ratio and re-circulation of exhaust, while still being able to achieve 110hp and a top speed of 105 mph (170 km/h) in its American version; but then all American cars were getting slower during these years. The 3-Series got its six-cylinder versions in 1977, with a 320-6 and fuel-injected 323i.

The 3-Series was the cheapest of the new range, the 316 originally selling at DM13,600. Between 1975 and 1978, 523,920 of these cars were produced, indicative of huge popularity. But the new line was far from complete. Having

Below: The two-door 3-Series is BMW's cheapest and best selling car, here seen in its 323i version.

Opposite page, right: The cockpit of the 323i. With the 3-Series, BMW began its exploration of ergonomically designed dashboards and driver positioning.

Opposite page, left: The 323i engine, which produces 143hp.

Above: The 635 CSi, posed at Munich's Olympic Stadium.

Below: The 628 CSi shows the full elegance of the 6-Series.

Far right: The engine of the 628 CSi.

already replaced and revamped its smaller four-cylinder two- and four-door cars and six-cylinder four-doors, BMW moved on to see how it could bring its six-cylinder coupés into line, particularly in order to supersede the 3.0 CS and CSi. The 630 CS/CSi, introduced in 1976, is a beautiful car: its vast windows give a bright and open look; the body is slung low and, in tune with the new style, is longer and wider than its predecessors. The wedge-shape shown when the car is seen in profile, derived from the Turbo and already partially incorporated in the 3-Series, is very accentuated in the 6-Series — it too was designed by Paul Bracq. The car also has a unique power-steering system (included as a standard feature) which is designed to diminish its effect regularly as speed increases, thus giving more feel of the road at high speeds. In terms of engine power, the 630 CS gives out 185hp and a top speed of 130mph (210km/h). A more powerful 633 CSi model was also introduced in 1976 and for the American market there was the 639 CSi with the same engine as the 530i. The most powerful car in this series was the 635 CSi brought out in 1978 with an engine based partly on the M1. The body is still the same except for spoilers, and is wider and lower than the rest of the series. It is the most sporty of the 6-Series cars, reflected in its slightly changed markings. Between 1976 and 1978, 16,277 of these cars were produced.

Finally, in 1977, came BMW's top-of-the-line 7-Series four-door sedans to replace the old 2500/2800 cars. Hugely expensive at upward of DM31,400 (1977 price), and directly competing with Mercedes again, the 7-Series is closely related to the 6-Series. The engine is six-cylinder, offered in three variations: 728, 730 and 733i (of which only the latter in modified version could be marketed in the USA). Basic design is identical to the 6-Series, but for the addition of a new front-suspension system based on a double-A-arm and new hydraulic brakes. The interior, with its highly evolved cockpit design, is lavish and even has a tool-kit built into its rear hood.

With the 7-Series in the showrooms, BMW had an extremely sensible range of cars to offer the consumer: only five body types, all unified through an idea of compact but practical comfort and performance; a prestigious car, but not an outlandish luxury. These five bodies now range from the sporty and small to the large, powerful, and substantial, spreading a net which has already caught huge and stable sales for over a decade. After a long and shaky history, BMW is finally and definitively here to stay.

By way of a postscript, we might look at BMW's one complete and certainly outlandish departure from the 3-7 Series logic, if only because it represents the BMW dream car that actually got to the production line: the M1, brought out in 1978. With a body designed by Giugiano's Ital Design, and most of its engineering by Lamborghini, the M1 was originally a racing car, which was produced as a road car for racing homologation. The M1 has a turbo-charged 3.5-liter six-cylinder engine mounted amidships, where it produces 277hp. None of it bears any resemblance to what one would identify with BMW, and at a price of DM100,000, it would hardly matter, anyway.

Opposite page, top: The interior of the 7-Series is built for total comfort.

Opposite page, bottom: Back view of a 733.

Below: The 7-Series is BMW's top of the line at present, a powerful and sleek four-door sedan.

Left: The M1 is BMW's current dream car, a formula racer which is on sale as a production model, but not seriously.

CHAPTER 6

BMW ON THE RACE TRACK

Of all automobile manufacturers, BMW boasts one of the longest and most consistent involvements in motor car competition. Starting right back in 1899, with a win for Wartburg in the Aachen-Koblenz distance race, Eisenach, and later BMW, have taken racing very seriously: it is no mere afterthought, but an integral part of what the company has been there to do.

For a manufacturer of quality, high-performance cars, this is not surprising. Winning races which test speed, handling and endurance is the very best form of advertising when a company is selling to drivers who like to think of themselves as kings of the road. For this reason it is also not surprising that BMW has only for very short periods in its history gone in for single-seater and non-production-model racing cars, choosing rather to run their regular models with far less than the usual modification; to win races with a car anyone could buy proves BMW's point in a way little else could. What is remarkable is BMW's adherence to this policy for upward of 80 years.

In the days of Eisenach's infancy, participation in reliability races was essential, being the only proving grounds for the new and untried vehicles. These races were very popular and constituted an important arena as they grabbed the attention of the motoring enthusiasts who could spread a car's reputation. Prior to the First World War, then, Wartburgs and Dixis were driven at many races, both by private and company-appointed drivers. To say that these were standard production models is somewhat less than meaningful at a time when so little standardization entered into motorcar manufacture. Suffice to say that, until after the war, there was little in the way of special racing body shapes, nor were the engines much modified. People just wanted to see what the cars could do, and in the early days that was enough.

The Dixis did well in competition, slowly building up a strong reputation for the company. In the 1907 Herkomer Trophy Trials, for example, four Dixi cars won gold plaques. In the Kaiser's Prize race in the Taunus Mountains, Dixi was established as Germany's third best maker of cars. Dixi was also successful in hill climbs: it was in all ways a robust and well-crafted car.

After the First World War, racing became more serious. So 6/18hp Dixis, often with modified engines, competed all over Germany, winning first and second places in the Grunewald Races in Berlin in 1921, second and third in the first Avus Race in 1921, and winning their class at Avus in 1922 (the winning car clocking up 69.2 mph (113.5 km/h)), while chalking up several wins in hill climbs and reliability runs. Also during this period, long-distance races were becoming regular annual events, and Dixis were equally regularly represented in them.

Dixi racing cars of the early 1920s were mainly 6/24s with four-cylinder 1568cc engines, giving out 39–40hp. Around 1923, 'streamlined' body shapes began appearing on these racers: these were usually tubular affairs, with flat

Above: A Wartburg Sport on the track.

Left: Wartburg Sports participating in the 1930 Eifelrennen.

Opposite page, top: In 1929, BMW 3/15s won the International Alpine Trials with an average speed of 25 mph (42 km/h).

front noses and pointed rear ends which looked like little missiles pointing backwards. In fact, Eisenach suffered in both racing and regular production from lack of a wind-tunnel, though it was very concerned about aerodynamics. This led to an interesting, if incidental, development. In 1923 the company commissioned a noted specialist engineer, Paul Jarry, to design a truly aerodynamic body for the Dixi. Though never produced, his result was very advanced for its time and certainly looked futuristic, unlike any other car produced until the 1950s.

In 1924 a 6/24 Dixi won the team prize in the 1840-km Reichsfahrt race, as well as several reliability runs and hill climbs – in all, 27 first and 17 second places. Two 6/24 Dixis also achieved an unofficial World Record, driving 20,000 km in 16 days on the Avus track. Another notable win was scored by Fritz Feuerstein, who took the 1925 Solitude race in a 6/24 Dixi.

As the company slid into its crisis period, it was less evident on the track, though private racers maintained some presence for Eisenach. But with the introduction of the 3/15 in 1927, Dixi, then BMW, made a remarkable comeback. It won first place in the 1928 Freiberg hill climb, as well as the Oberjoch, Baden-Baden, Klausenpass and Hohensyberg races. It also won the first four places in its class at the ADAC race on the Avus course in September 1928. One of its notable triumphs was to emerge as one of the only two teams to finish the gruelling 1928 International Alpine Tour without any penalty points. Finally, in the 3500-km economy test of the same year, the 3/15 got a third place.

The car's first major victory and the first racing triumph for BMW cars came in the form of the team prize at the 1929 International Alpine Trials, in which the 3/15s – modified to become 13/15 PSs – managed an average of 26 mph (42 km/h). This was followed by the little BMW winning its class at the 1930 Monte Carlo Rally, and by many more long-distance and hill-climb successes. A notable driver of 3/15s in this period was the police Lieutenant Knappe, who won the First International Police Rally in 1929, a 3000-km race to Hamburg; scored a seventh place overall in the 1931 Monte Carlo Rally, another long-distance drive; came first in his class in the 1931 Mont des Mules, for which his 3/15 was hailed as the Best German Car; and in the 1932 East Prussian Tour was one of only six cars to finish without penalty points. Knappe was, of course, a private racer, but had a long history with Dixi and BMW cars.

In 1934 the face of BMW racing was completely changed by the introduction of the 303, then the 315/1 and 319/1 to the race course. The latter two cars were supercharged versions of the 315 and 319 (but still available as regular production cars). Both were very successful and gave BMW a high profile on the tracks of the world. It was also the appearance of these three cars at the 1934 Alpine Trials that caught the eye of H J Aldington and led to the important association of BMW and Frazer Nash. BMW also won the team event at these trials. The new cars also brought BMW class wins in the 1934 2000-km Tour and the ADAC Reichsfahrt, which started from Eisenach. In 1935 there were many 315/1 and 319/1 wins.

However, a real milestone in BMW's prewar racing career was the dramatic debut of the 328 at the 1936 Eifelrennen — which it won, driven by Ernst Henne. The 328 — unlike other BMW cars — started life as a racer, and even when in production was turned out in very small numbers, only for the very sporty rich. In some races, the 328 went onto the track as it

Opposite page, top: A 1935 Frazer Nash/BMW 315.

Top: 328s totally dominated racing in the late 1930s, to the point that in this 2-liter race at the Nürburgring during the German Grand Prix of 1938, almost no other cars bothered to race.

Above: A 1939 Frazer Nash/BMW at Prescott in 1978.

came out of the factory. For the most part the engine was souped-up to produce 135hp and a top speed of 124 mph (200 km/h). To show what the 328 could do, 'Sammy' Davis, driving at Brooklands did 102.227 miles in one hour (164.59 km in an hour), a real feat for a 1936 two-liter. The car also won its first British race, the Tourist Trophy, and rapidly became the pace-setting car of its two-liter class. In the long run, it proved the most race-winning German car of those years. During 1936, the 328 won a string of races – Le Mans, the 24-hour race at Spa, Tourist Trophy, Mille Miglia, Avus, German Grand Prix, and even Mussolini's eccentric propaganda stunt, the Tobruk-Benghazi-Tripoli race.

Aside from class wins, the 328 picked up 5th, 7th, and 9th places overall at the 1939 Le Mans, easily winning its class and setting an amazing average speed of 82 mph (132 km/h); all three 328s finished the course, against a 50 percent finishing rate for the other marques.

But the 328's greatest hour came at the 1940 Mille Miglia, which raced to Brescia. Since 1938, BMW had been working to produce an aerodynamically efficient body for the 328, and had already raced new prototypes. One of these would have reached the assembly line by 1940 had peace continued. However, in the event, experimental versions of the aerodynamic coupé were entered in the 1940 Mille Miglia.

With engines producing up to 135hp, placed in featherlight space frames made of special metal (the whole car weighing 650 kg), these 328s took the race by storm. Of the five 328s which started the race, no less than four were included in the first six positions. Driver Fritz Huschke von Hanstein captured first place at a staggering average speed of 103.385 mph (166.45 km/h), and the other 328s took places three, five, and six. Unfortunately, the winning 328, as well as the other coupés that raced that day, are now lost.

In the years immediately following the war, no new cars were being produced for racing. As races resumed, the old prewar models returned to the tracks and the 328 therefore had several good years of competition ahead of it. One of the most successful drivers of this period was Alex von Falkenhausen, who raced his 328 throughout postwar Europe. Just as postwar firms copied BMW production models, so, too, many racing cars appeared in the late 1940s and early 1950s that were based on the 328's powerful engine (often reconstructed from salvaged parts). Most of these racers were oneoffs, privately built for drivers such as Hermann Holbein and Helmut Polensky. Many other Formula Three small car racers turned to BMW motorcycle engines. On the other hand, two firms turned out 328-based racers in some quantity: AFM and Veritas. Veritas, established by ex-BMW engineers,

produced almost exclusively for racing. Their cars were extremely light (520 kg) and streamlined and, with their highly-tuned 328 engines, were extremely fast. They made their debut at the Hockenheimring in 1947 and entered their first race, the Eggberg in 1948. They did moderately well before closing down in 1950.

Though 328s were kept racing in a low-key way throughout the 1950s (especially by von Falkenhausen), these years were as grim for BMW racing and rallying as for its normal production line. While most firms — and especially Mercedes — had long returned to their normal run of activities, BMW did not have the resources to produce a great showing on the track. Nonetheless, the company set up a racing department in 1954, with von Falkenhausen directing, and as they were producing powerful V8 cars in any case, these were entered into competition. In fact, everything BMW had, including Isettas and 600s, were rallied at one time or another. The 501s and 502s had some successes, but BMW racing was in eclipse during this decade and — as in the early days — relied largely on private drivers. In the 1954 ADAC winter rally, Ernst Loof (former head of Veritas) and Hans Wencher won the best time in a 501. At the last Mille Miglia ever held in 1957, BMW 502s achieved the best times for touring cars and obtained a class victory — just the sort of publicity they badly needed. However, the winning 502 was only 28th overall.

BMW's real return to racing — and return to automotive importance — began with the 700. This little car, with its light engine and body, excellent weight distribution, rack-and-pinion steering and superb handling, consistently outperformed cars with far larger engines. Starting with 30hp output from the original 700, up to 65hp were wrung from the 697cc engines of the later racing 700s. No wonder that,

well into the mid-1950s, rallies for under-700cc touring cars were dominated by this little BMW. The 700 was in a class of its own in hill climbs. In 1959, its first year, it managed 33 first and 22 second places and did just as well in 1960. The 700 maintained this dominance for some time. It was very much an international success: 700 class wins included the 1960 Alpine Trophy, Avus Rally, German Grand Prix, 12 Hours of Monza, 1962 and 1963 Rallye Acropolis, and the 1963 European Trophy for Touring Cars.

The era of the 700 lasted until around 1966; it was not until then that the New Class cars really began to enter the ring. Particularly important was a win by Hubert Hahne and Jacky Ickx in a 2000 ti at the 24 Hours of Spa. The 2002 began racing in 1968 and was as popular on the track as on the road. However, New Class cars never achieved the kind of status attained by the 700 in its class. One reason for this was that BMW itself had begun to concentrate almost exclusively on formula racing — a new departure. Prior to this, BMW's involvement with formula racing had been largely confined to supplying their superlative engines to other racers. Because of this new involvement, most New Class racing in the years around 1970 was by private entries, though some of the most noted drivers of BMWs such as

Opposite page: Brudes and Roese driving a BMW 328 during the 1940 Mille Miglia, in which BMW took places 1, 3, 5, and 6.

Above: A BMW 700 in the 1960 Alpine Rally. The 700s were a phenomenon in their class.

Left: A 2002 turbo on the track.

Hahne, Ickx, Siffert and Dieter Quester continued rallying BMW touring cars. The 2002 turbo, too, made a good impression.

Starting in 1971, BMW touring cars began making a real impact again. In that year, BMW scored a total of 87 class wins in closed circuit races and 92 in hill climbs. BMW put out its larger cars, mostly the 2800 CS, for the closed circuit races, and the 2002 ti proved highly competent on the hill climbs. In 1972, the team of Zweibaumen and Schons drove a BMW to become the German Rally Champions, while BMW racers also won championships in Denmark, Yugoslavia, Belgium, Austria, Italy, and several other countries. In 1973, the 3.0 CSL, driven by Hans Stuck and Chris Amon, won the Grand Prix for Touring Cars at the Nurburgring, and another BMW took second. Lauda, too, won with a BMW six-cylinder coupé at Monza in the same year. In 1974, Stuck drove a 3.0 CSL to a new record on the Nurburgring. In line with its return to racing production models, BMW began investing in making real sporting improvements in its touring cars over the next few years: these included incorporating rack-and-pinion steering and important aerodynamic developments.

In 1975, BMW started concentrating on North American events. In line with its normal role in racing, there were sound commercial reasons for this new interest: BMW had recently become embroiled in law suits with its long-time American distributor Hoffman Motors, and had set up its own distribution network. This would benefit from the support of large-scale promotional activities and BMW therefore entered the 3.0 CSL, in a souped-up racing version, in a full run of events — a success in sales terms if not top racing prizes.

Opposite page, top: BMW entered 3.0 CSLs in a string of North American events in the mid-1970s as part of its attempt to reorganize its American distribution system.

Opposite page, middle: A 2800 CS rounding the track.

Above: The 3.0 CSL was factory produced for racing homologation.

Left: In 1978, the BMW Junior Team headed by Giacomelli, won the Formula 2 European Championship.

In the mid-1970s, BMW commissioned several illustrious contemporary artists to hand paint racing 3.0 CSLs, which were then called *Kunstautos* and were unveiled at signing ceremonies and shown all over the world. Shown here are the works by (from left to right) Roy Lichtenstein, Frank Stella, and Alexander Calder.

INDEX

Acknowledgments
The author would like to thank the BMW Archive in Munich for their indefatigable help in locating pictures for this book. Herr Peter Zollner and Hans Fleischmann were especially helpful. All the photographs used in the book were supplied by BMW apart from the following:

Neill Bruce: pp 2–3, 28–9, 36 (both), 38–9 (all three), 88 (top), 88–9.
Geoffrey Goddard: pp 77 (top), 78–9, 79 (top), 80 (top), 80–1.